Olympic National Park

POCKET GUIDE

Levi T. Novey

FALCONGUIDES ®

GUILFORD, CONNECTICUT
HELENA, MONTANA

AN IMPRINT OF THE GLOBE PEQUOT PRESS

FACT SHEET

Park Features

Park size: 922,651 acres

Percent of park designated as wilderness: 95 (876,669 acres)

Visitation in 2006: 2,749,197

Visitation in 1938: 75,310

Number of named glaciers: 60 (third-largest glacial system in contiguous United States)

Miles of wilderness coast: 73

Miles of rivers and streams: More than 3,000

Number of trailheads: 64

Miles of trail: 611

Archaeological sites: More than 650 (50–70 permits for all kinds of research, including archaeological, biological, and historical, are issued annually)

Elevation at Hurricane Ridge: 5,242 feet

Highest Point: Mount Olympus (7,980 feet)

Precipitation: 200-plus inches of rain fall on Mount Olympus each year

Developed campgrounds: 16 (approximately 31,000 people camped overnight in the park's wilderness in 2005)

Plants and Animals

Endemic animals and plants: At least 16 kinds of endemic animals and 8 kinds of endemic plants

Endangered species: H to/used by 22 threatened endangered animal specie

History

Established as Mount Olympus National Monument o March 2, 1909.

Established as Olympic National Park on June 29, 1938.

Designated as an International Biosphere Reserv in 1976.

Designated as a World Heritage Site in 1981.

Some of this information was provided courtesy of Olympic National Park.

Contents

Welcome:
Introduction to Olympic National Park

For nature lovers, Olympic National Park's jewels are so splendid and diverse that they could well be the tale of a treasure hunter's wildest dreams. While most people who have studied maps will tell you that Olympic National Park is much like "three parks in one," they also might miss part of the big picture. Yes, it's true that Olympic has sizeable regions containing majestic snow-capped mountains, lush green forests with towering trees, and a wild coast with rocky, mysterious vistas that moan with the sea's audible whispers. The parts that many people miss in the "three parks in one" scenario are the rushing rivers, serene lakes, and glaciers that also play a big role in the experiences we can have as we explore the treasure-laden places within the park. Perhaps it's wiser to think of ourselves more as park stewards rather

Hurricane Ridge visitor center

than visitors—after all, it's important to remember that a group of thoughtful people helped protect these places so that we could enjoy them today.

Natural Features of the Park

Moving aside from such poetic claims and philosophical musings, what are the key things to know about the park's major regions? People often cite the park's rain forests as the feature that makes Olympic unique from other U.S. national parks. These rain forests are temperate and are quite different from tropical rain forests. Temperate rain forests, while quite biodiverse (abundant in their numbers of plant and animal species), don't come close to having the tremendous number of species that live in tropical rain forests. On the other hand, there is more biomass in Olympic temperate rain forests than in any other place in the world. Essentially this means that there is more living matter here by weight and bulk. Most of this matter lives in the form of plant life, such as mosses that thrive upon the abundant moisture as epiphytes: Plants that live upon other plants and often get their nutrients from the air. The one factor that makes temperate and tropical rain forests similar is the rain. Olympic National Park's rain forests receive an average of 135 inches annually. For comparison, Portland, Oregon, receives 36.3 inches per year; Atlanta, Georgia, gets 50.2 inches per year; and Boston, Massachusetts, soaks up 42.5 inches per year. The trees are quite large in the park's rain forest area.

The Hoh Rain Forest

and numerous champion trees for certain species live here. Some of these trees are almost a thousand years old. An important logistical note is that only the western half of Olympic National Park's forests are technically rain forests. The forests in the eastern sections of the park share many similar traits and are often mistaken as rain forests because they can look quite similar on the surface and are also potentially old-growth forests: forests that have old trees that are also characterized by a few key traits, such as enhanced ecosystem functions and increased biodiversity because of their age. The main difference between the rain forests of the park's western areas and the forests of the eastern areas (which both can be old growth) is the amount of rain they receive. These differences in moisture affect the types of plant species that can grow. Elevation also plays a role in which species grow where in the park.

Park Flora and Fauna

The Olympic Mountains are a distinct range from Washington's Cascade Mountains and were created by an isolated geological process that helped make the entire Olympic Peninsula unique. For this reason, some of Olympic National Park's animals and plants are found nowhere else in the world. Beyond the rain forest, this is a lesser-known but equally important reason why Olympic National Park is special: At least eight kinds of plants and fifteen kinds of animals live only on the Olympic Peninsula. One of the more famous of these animals is the Olympic marmot, which is only found in the

ew from Hurricane Ridge's Big Meadow Trail

Olympic Mountains, along with several species of endemic wildflowers, such as Piper's bellflower and Flett's violet. But aside from the animals and plants, most people journey into the Olympic Mountains to see incredible landscapes and viewpoints. Many park visitors take the winding, 17-mile mountain road to Hurricane Ridge, where a visitor center overlooks one of the most awesome panoramic views of the Olympic peaks. The tallest is Mount Olympus at 7,980 feet (but it's hard to distinguish from the view at Hurricane Ridge). Few people come here in the summer without taking at least a short hike to get more views and see how some of the trees and plants, like the common subalpine fir and late-spring glacier lily, have adapted to the harsher winter weather conditions. In the colder months, Hurricane Ridge is

sometimes open on weekends if condi-tions permit, and you can snowshoe or cross-country ski to enjoy the winter landscapes.

Farther west of the Olympic Moun-tains are the Pacific Ocean and the wild Olympic Coast. Large erosion-resistant rocks in the ocean, known as sea stacks

Sea anemones wait for prey.

the beaches, alternately seeming like
⸻ers of the ocean's movement at high
⸻ and as mysterious giants looming in
distance when the coast is cloudy.
⸻en near these sea stacks and the
⸻aller coves that surround them you
⸻ find tide pools, where hundreds of
⸻all sea creatures, such as sea stars
⸻rfish), sea anemones, and limpets,
⸻le for survival despite their serene
⸻earance. Lucky wanderers will some-
⸻es see sea lions resting on the sandy
⸻res, bald eagles and brown pelicans
⸻sting across the water looking for
⸻, or sea otters foraging out in the surf.
⸻ arches, holes, and spires carved in
⸻he of the large rocks by water over
⸻e are striking locations for taking pic-
⸻es. Large pieces of driftwood roll out
⸻n the rivers and into the ocean, only
⸻nd up back on the shore abutting the

Sea otters can be seen foraging on the coast.

coastal forests—further illustrating the
ocean's power. There are also places like
Ozette, where some of the peninsula's
earlier human inhabitants created art-
work that has lasted, despite having one
of their coastal communities buried by a
terrifying tsunami.

Glaciers and Waterways

While few visitors see the park's glaciers (except perhaps from a distance), they feed the rivers, streams, waterfalls, and lakes with fresh water and a cycle of rebirth, perhaps best manifested by the likes of species such as salmon, which spawn in the rivers and provide other animals with sustenance. A lack of nitrogen makes the waters of Lake Crescent clear, while the large Ozette Lake, and the nearby locations of Lake Quinault and Lake Cushman, also attract park visitors. There is also an abundance of smaller lakes. Numerous rivers travel out from the Olympic Mountains, like rays from a child's drawing of the sun, while other tributaries meander through other areas in the park like less-polished scribbles. Waterfalls are common and a favorite with visitors.

A Pristine Wilderness

So after reading about all of these features of Olympic National Park, such as its diversity in landscapes and its unique plant and animal species, it's not hard to imagine how these pieces of the park are interconnected, and that these connections help make each individual ecosystem complete. Because of these connections and also to protect its pristine natural resources, about 95 percent of the park's 922,651 acres are designated as wilderness—areas where people are legally mandated to have as little impact as possible. Also, no roads traverse the park, making the protection of natural resources easier; people are limited to accessing the park via trailheads and numerous roads that lead in and out of the park. The park's

Lake Cresce

biodiversity and relatively ecologically intact systems make it an important place for scientific research and education. Several current studies include an investigation of the movement pattern of black bears and the reasons for the apparent population decline among Olympic marmots.

It's hard to visit every part of the park in only a few days, but there are numerous ways—including sightseeing, hiking, beachcombing, swimming, boating, fishing, and camping—to make your time in the park memorable and fun. The chapters that follow provide more details about getting around the park, the park's animals and plants, its history, park activities, lodging and dining, and a few tips.

Park researchers at work

Navigate:
Getting to and around the park

Olympic National Park is so big that to circle the borders of the inland portion of the park, it would take at least eight hours of driving, without even entering the in/out roads that allow you to see the park itself. Most people arrive to Olympic National Park by car, either traveling from the Seattle area or from Washington's southern regions. A small airport is located in Port Angeles, the primary gateway city to the park, although most people fly into the Seattle area and then rent a car. There is little in the way of public transportation available on the peninsula, although there is a bus system with an infrequent schedule that is used primarily by locals. A ferry travels regularly to and from Port Angeles, but its sole destination is Victoria, Canada, a popular tourist destination (the ferry readily transports cars). Most people coming from the Seattle area first head to

An interpretive program at the Port Angeles visitor center

Getting There

Getting to Port Angeles from the Seattle area takes about three hours on average. There are two primary routes to take from Seattle. The first takes you on one several ferries that cross the Puget Sound from the Seattle area. After disembarking, you then drive the rest of the way to Port Angeles. Ferry fees currently are about $15 one way for a car and its driver and $7 for each additional passenger. Ferries come and go often, but sometimes there can be long waits depending on passenger volume. For more information about ferry schedules and fees, visit www.wsdot.wa.gov/ferries. The second route involves driving south on Interstate 5, and then taking U.S. Highway 16 in Tacoma to U.S. Highway 3, to Highway 104, and then to U.S. Highway 101. So

Port Angeles, because this is where the park's primary visitor center is located, as well as the only roads to the mountains and the highway that leads to the park's other major areas.

:h route is faster? It depends on traf-
ime of year, time of day, and a lot of
. The lower-stress option is to take a
, because it's fun if it's not something
've done frequently. You might see
ohins or harbor seals from the ferry's
<s or windows, as well as get some
views of Seattle. The downside
at you are probably more likely to
nd extra time and money going this
Of course, the roads are typically a
more reliable time-wise and a tad
expensive. But if driving in heavy traf-
nd paying attention for where to turn
your idea of a good time, perhaps a
more dollars and minutes isn't that
of a price to pay.

tting Around

e on the Olympic Peninsula, US 101
e major road that takes you to the

park's different areas. Many people start
at the park's primary visitor center in
Port Angeles to get information, view
exhibits, and obtain a weather report
for Hurricane Ridge, the most weather-
dependent place in the park to visit
year-round. It's about a forty-five-minute
drive up a winding road, so if the view
from Hurricane Ridge is obstructed—a
possibility on cloudy and rainy summer
days—visitors like to know ahead of
time. The weather up on Hurricane Ridge
has surprisingly little relationship with
the weather down in Port Angeles. If you
have a couple days, you might pass on
Hurricane Ridge if its weather isn't ideal
and instead head in the direction of Lake
Crescent, the rain forests, the rivers, or
the coast. Lake Crescent, only about
thirty minutes from Port Angeles, is a
popular destination for those who have

Hurricane Ridge on a cloudy day

Park Entrances, Fees, and Visitor Centers

Entrance stations to the park are located at Heart of the Hills (on the way to Hurricane Ridge), Elwha, Sol Duc, Ozette, Staircase, and Hoh. Entrance fees currently are about $15 for a vehicle and all of its passengers but are likely to rise in upcoming years to around $25. The pass is good for a week. An annual pass is available for a higher fee. Entrances are open twenty-four hours a day during most of times of year, but they're not always staffed (some areas also close the winter months).

There are numerous visitor centers and ranger information stations in the park (generally open and staffed daily from 9:00 a.m. to 5:00 p.m. in the summer). The primary visitor center in

little time to spend in the park. Many people on tight time schedules are disappointed to learn that to see the authentic rain forest, one must travel two hours one way from Port Angeles. Many of the old-growth forests can just as easily appear to be rain forests to untrained eyes, however, and the Heart of the Hills area near the Port Angeles visitor center has one such old-growth forest.

t Angeles has the most information
 exhibits and the largest bookstore.
 so shows a popular film about the
k. Staff members are readily avail-
e to answer questions and help you

Rainy Day?
Take a Waterfall Tour!

On days when the weather at
Hurricane Ridge isn't great, many
people opt to take a tour of three
waterfalls in the park. (Even if
it's raining, you'll stay fairly dry
in the forests.) Madison Falls is
just a short walk from a parking
area, and Marymere and Sol Duc
Falls are each easy 1-mile walks
through the forest.

plan your activities. Other large visitor
centers are located at Hurricane Ridge,
in Forks, in the Hoh Rain Forest, and at
Lake Quinault. While not a visitor center,
the Wilderness Information Center,
located next to the visitor center in Port
Angeles, is an important place. People
who plan to go backpacking overnight in
the park's backcountry are required to
register here and pick up their permits.
If the backcountry campsite that will be
used doesn't have a device for storing
food away from animals, bear canisters
are strongly recommended and are
offered for free (donation suggested).
Wilderness Information Center staff
are also experts on trails and staying
overnight in the park, and they can offer
tips and maps. Numerous other ranger
information stations and kiosks are
located throughout the rest of the park,

How Long Does It Take to Drive from _____ to _____ ?

Seattle to Port Angeles via ferry: 3 hours, 72 miles
Sea-Tac Airport to Port Angeles via Tacoma: 3 hours, 170 miles
Port Angeles to Deer Park: 45 minutes, 18 miles
Port Angeles to Hurricane Ridge: 45 minutes, 17 miles
Port Angeles to Lake Crescent (Barnes Point): 30 minutes, 20 miles
Port Angeles to Forks: 1 hour 15 minutes, 59 miles
Port Angeles to Hoh Rain Forest: 2 hours, 91 miles
Port Angeles to Ozette: 2 hours 30 minutes, 88 miles
Port Angeles to Mora: 1 hour 35 minutes, 73 miles
Port Angeles to Kalaloch: 2 hours, 95 miles
Sol Duc to Forks: 50 minutes, 39 miles
Forks to Hoh Rain Forest: 45 minutes, 32 miles
Forks to Kalaloch: 45 minutes, 36 miles
Forks to Mora: 20 minutes, 14 miles
Lake Crescent to Sol Duc: 45 minutes, 23 miles
Lake Crescent to Forks: 45 minutes, 37 miles
Kalaloch to Quinault Rain Forest: 45 minutes, 33 miles
Quinault to Staircase: 3 hours, 120 miles
Quinault to Sea-Tac Airport: 3 hours, 141 miles
Staircase to Port Angeles: 3 hours, 100 miles

ough they are inconsistently staffed, e varying degrees of information, and cally have fewer items for sale in their kstores.

Aside from the visitor center at ricane Ridge, and several places at e Crescent and Lake Quinault, it is d to find places to buy food and sup- s in the park. Just outside the bound- s, however, there are towns where can purchase gas, supplies, and d. Port Angeles, Sequim, Forks, and dsport offer the most businesses services, although you will also find tes sprinkled throughout other areas vell.

rk Regulations d Safety

k regulations are extensive concern- camping, hiking, fishing, vehicle use,

collection of plants and berries, and general use of the park. One worth men- tioning in more detail is that pets are only allowed in campgrounds and in parking lots on leashes, and on a few short spans of beach on the coast. Cougars (also known as mountain lions) roam through- out the park (even on the coast) and are sometimes attracted to pets, putting you and your pet in danger. Pets can also disturb and threaten wildlife protected in the park. If you have a pet and want to take it on trails, the Olympic National For- est that surrounds park areas provides opportunities to do so.

Animals in the park, such as black bears, cougars, mountain goats, deer, and elk, can be dangerous if provoked or threatened. Most of the animals don't have great interest in our regular activities, however, because of the park's efforts to educate visitors and prevent negative human-animal interactions in the park (such as the proper storage of food at campgrounds). If you're concerned about how to act if you see one of these large animals, there are a number of sources to consult throughout the park, and information is generally posted in areas with frequent cougar and bear activity. Generally speaking, the best thing to do is keep a safe distance from any of these animals.

For your safety, note that weather can change rapidly year-round, so bring appropriate clothing for a range of conditions, particularly rain. Even in the summer, it can be slightly chilly, with average temperatures ranging from 65 to 75 degrees Fahrenheit. In winter, sometimes certain areas will be shut down due to snow and unfavorable conditions.

Olympic National Park Contact Information
Address: 600 East Park Avenue, Port Angeles, WA 98362-6798
Web site: www.nps.gov/olym
Visitor information: (360) 565-313•
Road and weather hotline: (360) 565-3131
Wilderness Information Center/ backcountry permits: (360) 565-3100

Finally, it is also important to be aware of the tide schedule on the coa• (At high tide you can quickly become trapped against the rocks and forest.) Tide schedules are generally available local phone books and are posted on • letin boards in coastal areas of the par•

History:
Key things about the park

The Birth of the Olympics

Although we tend to think of history as being about things that happened in the past, many of its events lead to what we see and experience in the present. This might seem like an eloquent way of stating the obvious, but in Olympic National Park there are everyday reminders of what happened in the past, as a result of natural forces and people. These events are not just in the past but are usually ongoing. For instance, if you see one of the park's endemic species in the mountains, such as the Olympic yellow-pine chipmunk, you might ponder how more than thirty-five million years ago, this chipmunk would have been drowning under the ocean's waves. Around that time, the tectonic plate that carried the ocean floor crashed into the terrestrial plate of what we now think of as Washington, driving the ocean plate below the earth through a geological process known as subduction. This powerful collision pushed some of the plate upward though, in essence creating the precursor for the Olympic Mountains. Later, in the Ice Age, glacial sheets pushed and carved the water channels that became the Puget Sound and the Strait of Juan de Fuca. These glacial masses isolated the Olympic Peninsula from the remainder of the mainland, leaving the species present at that time on the peninsula to evolve, while leaving other species like mountain goats behind. This isolation is the reason why the Olympic chipmunks, and other endemic species we see today in the park, are unique.

Weather patterns also play a role in the landscape. While the process of subduction continues today, and we wou[ld] thus assume the Olympics would be pushed higher, the net gain is basically zero. Rain and wind moving onshore from the coast erode the mountain to[p] at the same rate as they rise. Weather patterns also force air and moisture to different places, effectively creating microclimates as well as a rain shadow on the Olympic Peninsula, allowing different plant species to grow. The east[ern] Olympics are in this rain shadow and receive considerably less moisture tha[n] the western and central areas, as the cold air and lowering air pressure forc[e] most moisture down as rain or snow a[t] places like Mount Olympus and Hurricane Ridge. To help indicate what a difference the rain shadow makes, prickl[y] pear cactuses are sometimes seen in t[he] rain shadow areas.

Early People

Probably around 12,000 years ago, as the glaciers retreated, people arrived the Olympic Peninsula. They hunted and gathered while exploring and building homes and making communities. Distinct cultures began to develop with strong dependence upon and appreciation for nature. Today there are at least eight tribes with historic ties to lands in Olympic National Park: the Elwha Klallam, Hoh, Jamestown S'Klallam, Makah, Port Gamble S'Klallam, Quileute, Quinault, and Skokomish. Their influence on the peninsula's modern cultural landscape is unquestionable, and their cultures are rich and vibrant despite the challenges they faced with the arrival Euro-American peoples. An annual InterTribal Canoe Journey to a different tribal community each year thrills and

The 2005 InterTribal Canoe Journey finished in Port Angeles.

inspires members of the tribes to actively embrace their heritage and is followed by a weeklong celebration with dances, food, and music.

The Arrival of European Explorers

Juan de Fuca, a Greek sea captain exploring for Spain in 1592, was probably the first European to see the Olympic Peninsula. More explorers followed, and much later in 1788 English explorer Capt. John Meares saw a towering mountain that reminded him of the home of the Greek gods. He chose a name that stuck: Mount Olympus. In the mid-1850s Euro-American settlers came to the peninsula, and toward the end of the century, explorers began to journey through the interior of what to them were the "unknown" Olympic Mountains.

The most notable of these explorers were Lieut. Joseph O'Neil, who eventually advocated for the creation of a national park, and the Press Expedition, a group funded by the *Seattle Press* newspaper who were the first Euro-Americans to document crossing the Olympics from north to south. Several historic homesteads and cabins still

"It has no geysers but every other requisite for a national park, as many wonders and natural beauties as can be found in any localities . . ."

—LIEUT. JOSEPH P. O'NEIL, 189(

remain in some areas of the park, such as Humes Ranch in the Elwha and Kest ner Homestead in the Quinault.

Logging and Conservatio

Logging and the unchecked use of forests on the peninsula became a major issue as early as the 1890s. As a result President Grover Cleveland created the Olympic Forest Reserve in 1897. Despi the protection, only several years

...ers explore Humes Ranch.

Olympic elk rest along the Hoh River.

later Olympic elk populations critically decreased because of overhunting. President Theodore Roosevelt, who followed soon after Cleveland, was a serious conservationist and took matters into his own hands. He redesignated some of the lands in the reserve as Olympic National Monument in 1909. There was a backlash, and the lands protected by the monument were decreased just a few years later—leaving forests in per again. In 1938 this trend was reversed, and Olympic was once more redesigna ted—this time as a national park. Presi dent Franklin Roosevelt had toured the peninsula a year earlier and chosen to support the protection of the forests.

The battle is still not over between pro- and anti-logging advocates, how- ever. The controversy reached a fever pitch in the early 1990s as one animal, the northern spotted owl, became a symbol of our growing understanding the fragility of ecosystems. It was liste as an endangered species—dealing a major blow to the logging industry. Sp ted owl populations reached this statu due to their dependence on a decreas number of old-growth forests for their source of food, which consists primari of northern flying squirrels. (The squir-

controversy-inspiring northern spotted owl

rels also tend to live in old-growth forests because it's where they can find and dine on truffles: the fruiting bodies of underground fungi that only begin to grow in trees' root systems after hundreds of years.) The spotted owl's predicament is also hastened by the encroachment of nonnative barred owls, which compete with the spotted owls for nesting spaces.

Looking to the Future: Park Restoration

The second-largest ecological restoration project in National Park Service history is currently taking place in Olympic National Park. In the 1910s and 1920s, on the Elwha River two hydroelectric dams were constructed, but without fish ladders (passageways for fish to swim upstream). As a result, one of the richest, most abundant salmon communities in the

The Lower Elwha Dam will soon be removed.

United States declined. At least 137 species of wildlife use salmon for sustenance in some way, and the decline altered the river ecosystem's integrity, as well as the Elwha Tribe's traditional harvesting grounds. In 1992 the U.S. Congress passed an act that authorized Elwha River Dam Removal and Ecosystem Restoration. The park has purchased the dams and in cooperation with the Elwha Tribe and various other groups and agencies plans to remove them and restore the ecosystem. Dam removal is scheduled begin in the near future, and we will be witness to history being made.

Flora and Fauna:
All things great and small

Olympic National Park impresses with its biodiversity, being the home to numerous plant and animal species. Starting with the animals, there are sixty-two terrestrial species of mammals, and twenty-four additional mammals that live in or use the ocean. Predacious weasels known as fishers once lived in the Olympics and will probably be reintroduced in the upcoming years, adding to the total. Reintroducing wolves has also been discussed, but it seems less likely to occur, at least in the near future. There are 20 reptile and amphibian species, 37 native fish species, and around 300 bird species in the park. Invertebrate species are too numerous to count. Each animal has interesting traits and stories to tell.

Fauna

Black Bear

While there are no grizzly bears in Olympic National Park, there are black bears. They range throughout all of Olympic's habitats, but you're lucky if you see one. For several years the park and the U.S. Geological Service have been researching the movement patterns of bears in the park's Elwha region. Data is currently collected by using hair snags to understand bear diet and to obtain an estimate of the minimum bear population. The goal is to understand how black bear movement patterns might change after the Elwha River ecosystem is restored in the years following the dam's removal. It's hoped that once native salmon are able to return and spawn upstream, bears and other animals will use the Elwha more frequently.

Olympic Marmot

Research has also been occurring for some time to understand more about Olympic marmots. They are one of the park's sixteen species of unique, endemic animals, and a recently apparent population decline has concerned park staff and scientists. Early findings suggest that these furry, large rodents that live in burrows in the ground have

The endemic Olympic marmot

under increased hunting pressure predators, such as coyotes, which not native to the marmots' ecosys-. The marmots only have about three our months to eat, breed, and raise young because they hibernate in winter, when weather is harsh. For reason, coming out in the open at s in the summer and spring is a essity for survival—and makes them erable to predators.

untain Goat

ntain goats, while native to the Cas- e Mountains of Washington, were not nally part of the Olympic ecosystem ause of its historic geological isola- from the rest of the state. While this wed unique species to evolve in the , it also meant that some species, goats, were excluded. Mountain

Introduced in the 1920s, mountain goats are not native to the park.

goats were introduced to the park in the 1920s, before it was understood that they might have a negative effect on some plant species that had evolved without them—specifically some of Olympic's endemic species, such as the Flett's violet. For this reason, a controversial effort was made to remove the goats by live capture using helicopters in the 1980s, with mixed success. Since that time a number of alternatives have been proposed, but it's a charged issue: Many would like to see the goats stay. Goat populations in the park are currently being monitored, and the scientific data will be used to make future management decisions.

Banana Slug

Within the park's forests you can often see banana slugs after it rains. These

slimy mollusks have no shells and del park visitors with their banana-like appearance. They are adept at using their slime in a variety of ways, such a to lower themselves from high branch and to escape from predators. If you dare touch one, know that the slime is notoriously challenging to remove. Despite their slick moving ways, bana

While quite slow, banana slugs are interestin forest creatures.

s help recycle leaf litter on the forest
r, and for that reason they play a
cial role in the ecosystem.

Life

 pools on the coast are home to a
ber of interesting creatures, such
ea stars (starfish), sea anemones,
ets, and clams. Sea stars, while best
wn for their shape, are here actually
ous predators of animals like clams.
 take hold of the clam from its shell,
mpt to unhinge it, and then grab
le with a leg to collect their prize.
anemones are also predators and
 for algal feeders like limpets and
 small fish to float by. They sting
n with their tentacles before devour-
hem.
 Finally, there are twenty-two animal
ies listed as "threatened" or "endan-

A sea star in a tide pool

gered" that are found in and around
Olympic National Park. This underscores
the importance of the park's role as a
safe haven and its goal to protect them.

Which Animals Am I Most Likely to See in the Park, and Where?

Animal	Likelihood	Location/Viewing Tips
Bears	Low	Mountains, backcountry, and quieter roads. Use binoculars from Hurricane Ridge and Hurricane Hill to spot in nearby areas.
Elk	Low	Rain forests, particularly along road to Hoh and near Bunch Falls in Quinault.
Deer	High	Anywhere along roads.
Pileated woodpeckers	Medium	Forests. Listen for distinctive Woody Woodpecker call and pecking noises while scanning trees.
Bald eagles	Medium	Coastal areas, particularly near La Push and Rialto Beach. Immature eagles have brown heads.
Marmots	Medium	Mountains in backcountry, and also Hurricane Hill and Obstruction Point Road.
Banana slugs	High	Forests. Look in moist areas and on logs.
Salmon	Medium	Look down in rivers in calm areas, particularly in the fall.
Sea otters	Low	On the coast, sometimes seen near Cape Alava and Rialto Beach.
Harbor seals	Medium	Look in saltwater areas on the coast and in harbors along Strait of Juan de Fuca.

*eagles are common along the Olympic
...st.*

Flora

There are more than 1,200 types of plants in the park, and most prominent among them are the tall trees, which range from hundreds to thousands of years old. The forests are so tight for space that any fallen tree becomes a host, or nurse log, for seedlings of the lucky species that land there. Old snags, dead trees that are still standing, provide homes for animals such as squirrels and woodpeckers. One of the giant species, the Douglas fir, is dependent upon fire for its seeds to sprout, and large fires have traditionally occurred in cycles of every hundred years in the park. Other large species include the western hemlock, western red cedar (easily identified by its distinctive bark), and the Sitka spruce, which seems to need either the high moisture or grazing elk—or both—that

Tall trees in the Hoh Rain Forest

only the rain forests tend to provide. I the mountains, subalpine firs dominat the landscape, reproducing via cones also a process called "layering" where they can sprout new trees from branc in contact with the ground. These tree provide a buffer from the harsh winter winds and snow and allow the firs to survive at higher elevations. Smaller plants such as shrubs, wildflowers, fer mosses, and lichens are no less intere ing. For instance, skunk cabbage has large green leaves and yellow flowers, and its odor—which smells like what y would imagine—attracts pollinators. T honey dew's colorful flowers and swee smell also attract insects, but it traps and devours them. The short pendent moss only starts growing after a forest around 200 years old, at the top of lim in the forest canopy. A threatened coa

, the marbled murrelet, nests on
kind of moss, and for this reason it's
endent on old-growth forests. It was
last bird in North America to have its
: discovered (because who looks at
top of the inland forest canopy for a
stal bird's nest?) The connections are
r: Each animal and plant in the park
a role, and if a few pieces start to dis-
ear, so might others. This is why the
tection the park provides is crucial.

Summer wildflowers in the Olympic Mountains

Horizons:
Natural and historic sites

This chapter provides a little more detail about each of the park's major areas marked on the map. Hiking trails are sometimes mentioned here but are covered more substantially in the Get Going chapter. Beginning with the northeast area known as Deer Park, we'll work our way counterclockwise around the park.

Deer Park

Deer Park is in the mountains and rain shadow of Olympic National Park, and a long, winding, unpaved mountain road leads to it from eastern Port Angeles. The views here are different from those you get at Hurricane Ridge, and a short trail leads from a parking area up

◀ *Sunset and clouds at Deer Park*

to the top of Blue Mountain (6,007 feet), which gives a nice view of the Strait of Juan de Fuca and surrounding areas. A couple other trails lead into the mountains, including the popular Grand Ridge Trail that leads to Obstruction Point. A primitive campground here is quite nice and peaceful, and as you might guess, deer are frequent visitors.

Hurricane Ridge

Next up is the aforementioned Hurricane Ridge area, which has a great view of the mountains from its visitor center. The area gets its name from the hurricane-force winds of up to 75 mph that sometimes gust here in winter. An average of 30 to 35 feet of snow drops each year, demanding that the plants and animals either depart, die, or adapt. The ridge is the starting point for a lot of shorter and

longer trails that lead you to beautiful subalpine views and encounters with wildflowers, wildlife, and nature. In the winter, snow and a small downhill-ski operation attract visitors when conditions permit. A scenic unpaved road leads from the visitor center parking lot to Obstruction Point, where several more popular trailheads take hikers deeper into the mountains and to subalpine lakes and valleys. (*NOTE:* The road may be scary for some.)

Elwha Area

Heading farther west, the Elwha area is poised to become world-famous because of the Elwha dam removal project and river ecosystem restoration (discussed more in the History chapter).

◀ *A winter view from Hurricane Ridge*

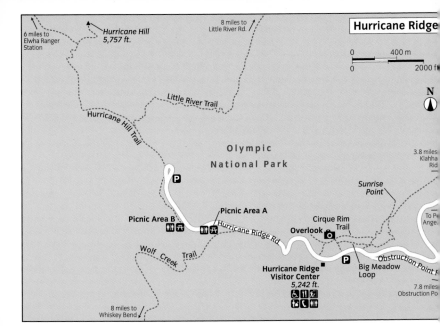

Elwha Valley

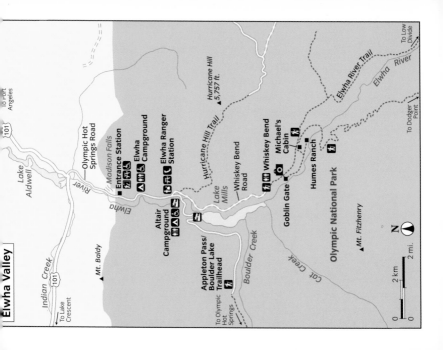

The river as we see it now is nonetheless beautiful and clear. The Elwha valley and river corridor were historically used by the Elwha Tribe for hunting and gathering, and later by Euro-American settlers as places to make cabins and homesteads. Some of these historic buildings can still be seen today. A number of campgrounds and an assortment of trails are here, including the Elwha River Trail, which takes backpackers across the park from north to south over an average of five days. The Olympic Hot Springs, the park's only undeveloped hot springs, is located in this area as well.

Lake Crescent

Next, heading west, is Lake Crescent. A lack of nitrogen in the lake prevents serious algal growth and makes the lake's water extremely clear. The lake, if viewed from above, is shaped like a crescent moon. Soothing environs make it popular for swimming, boating, fishing, and relaxing. A resort and lodge are located on the north and south sides of the lake and a campground on the west. The lake's geological history and isolation have made it home to genetically distinct varieties of rainbow and cutthroat trout that are known respectively as Beardslee and Crescenti trout. The lake's trails, the gorgeous old-growth forests that surround it, and its proximity to Marymere Falls seal the deal, making it a must-see location in the park.

Sol Duc River Area

The Sol Duc River glides out to the ocean from the interior of the Olympics, and in the fall, salmon often can be seen swimming upstream to spawn. The forests

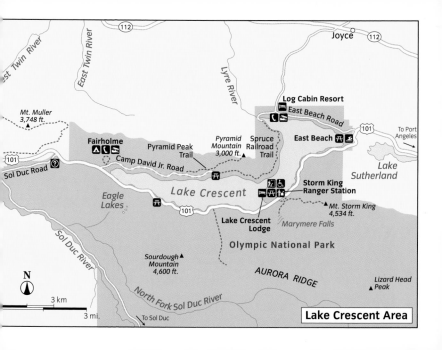

Lake Crescent Area

Joyce

112

East Twin River

East Twin River

Lyre River

To Port Angeles

101

Log Cabin Resort

East Beach Road

East Beach

Lake Sutherland

Mt. Muller
3,748 ft.

Fairholme

Pyramid Peak Trail

Pyramid Mountain
3,000 ft.

Spruce Railroad Trail

101

Sol Duc Road

Camp David Jr. Road

Lake Crescent

Storm King Ranger Station

Mt. Storm King
4,534 ft.

Eagle Lakes

101

Lake Crescent Lodge

Marymere Falls

Olympic National Park

Sol Duc River

Sourdough Mountain
4,600 ft.

AURORA RIDGE

Lizard Head Peak

N

3 km

3 mi.

North Fork Sol Duc River

To Sol Duc

Sol Duc Falls

around the Sol Duc are quite old, and when combined with the interesting S Duc Falls and Sol Duc Hot Springs, it's no wonder that this place has one of the most popular campgrounds in the park and that there is a developed res at the hot springs. The falls are a shor hike through old-growth forest, and th developed hot springs are open to the public for a small fee. The easiest acc to the popular backpacking-destinatic region referred to both as the Seven Lakes Basin and the High Divide is als Sol Duc.

Ozette Area

Within the coastal region of the park, the farthest area north is known as Ozette. A small campground lies on th north end of Lake Ozette, and this are was once popular with Euro-Americar

ers. Today, the area is well known for
-mile round-trip, triangle-shaped hike
ugh coastal forests along board-
s to Cape Alava and Sandpoint.
e petroglyphs, or rock art, from ear-
ribal inhabitants of the coast can be
d in a certain area near Cape Alava.
eral hundred years ago, on Cape
a's north end, a coastal village lived
ancestors of the Makah Tribe was
ered entirely by mud slides triggered
massive tsunami. The covered vil-
was discovered in 1970 and became
rld-famous archaeological site.
y of the items obtained from the
are now in the Makah Museum. To
orth of Cape Alava, two interesting
tal locations worth noting are Shi
Beach, an oft written about scenic
tion, and also Point of the Arches,
re rocky arches at the water's edge

make for interesting viewing and photographs. These locations are most easily
accessed through the Makah Reservation to the north and require considerable hiking.

Mora and La Push

In the central area of the park's coastal
region are the Mora and La Push areas.
While these areas are geographically
next to each other, they are split by the
Quillayute River and are reached by
separate roads. At Mora there is a park
campground, several trails, and the
popular Rialto Beach. It is probably the
closest coastal area to Port Angeles. A
flat 1.5-mile hike along the beach leads
to Hole-in-the-Wall, where tide pools
can be seen at low tide in and around a
large arching hole in a rock. La Push is
the principal community on the Quileute

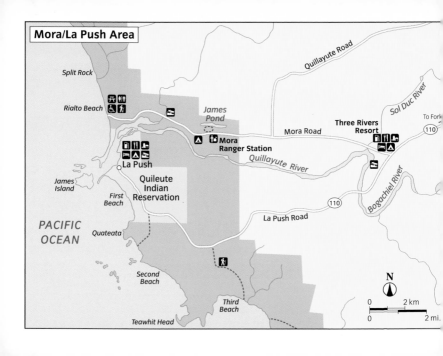

Mora/La Push Area

Split Rock

Rialto Beach

James Pond

Quillayute Road

Sol Duc River

Three Rivers Resort

Mora Road

To Forks

110

Mora
Ranger Station

La Push

James
Island

First
Beach

*Quileute
Indian
Reservation*

Quillayute River

Bogachiel River

110

La Push Road

**PACIFIC
OCEAN**

Quateata

Second
Beach

Third
Beach

Teawhit Head

N

0   2 km

0   2 mi.

in-the-Wall is easy to get to from Rialto Beach.

Indian Reservation, and via this area the Quileute grant visitors access to a charming set of numbered beaches in the park. They are individually known as First, Second, and Third Beach.

Hoh Rain Forest

Moving back east, the Hoh Rain Forest is a favorite spot for visitors. A moss-covered phone booth near the visitor center wows the uninitiated from the start. Two short loop trails, the Hall of Mosses and Spruce Nature Trails, are what most people take to see the rain forest and its majestic, towering trees and lush plants. Each trail is relatively flat and close to a mile round-trip. A long 18-mile hike starting from here is also is the primary route that leads backpackers to Mount Olympus. It travels along the Hoh River through the rain

The Hall of Mosses Trail

st. A beautiful campground delights rnighters and is located near the or center. If you want to see Olympic the Hoh is one of the best places in park to be on the lookout for them, ough they can be quite elusive.

laloch

southernmost area of the park's st is Kalaloch, which means "a good e to land" in the Quinault Tribe's uage. The only park campground ted directly on a beach is here, for this reason it is the only park pground with a reservation sys-. Spots book up early. A lodge also ides accommodations, as well as a aurant. Ruby Beach is a big draw as it sy to reach and has some sea stacks tide pools.

Tall-Tree Sighting

There are many places where you can see large and tall trees in the park's forests. In addition to stops along the roads in the Hoh, Kalaloch, and Quinault, you can easily access some on the Heart of the Forest Trail near Port Angeles, the Marymere Falls Trail at Lake Crescent, the Hall of Mosses Trail in the Hoh, and the Sol Duc Falls Trail in Sol Duc.

Queets

Moving back inland, the Queets area of the park is in the rain forest and is quieter and less frequented. A road follows along the Queets River and leads to a primitive campground that has a trailhead. This area doesn't offer much in the way of services or places to stop, and it's mainly frequented by parkgoers interested in fishing, hiking, backpacking, or camping. The road is washed out, and checking for bypass routes is strongly advised.

Quinault

Farther east of Queets is the southern park area of Quinault, where a historic lodge sits on the east side of the large lake of the same name. Rain forests bound the lake on both sides. Confusing to visitors is that the U.S. Forest Service manages the area on the east side of the lake, and the National Park Service manages the area on the west side. There are also many private homes here. Beyond the lake, roads lead through the rain forest to a primitive campground as well as trailheads, which lead into the park deep interior wilderness to such places as the Enchanted Valley, where a number of cascades sometimes fall from the mountains in the spring and summer.

Staircase

Staircase, located in the park's south-eastern corner just above the north end of Lake Cushman, is one of the closer areas for hikers and campers coming from the Seattle area. The North Fork the Skokomish River cascades through the forest here, and a common misconception is that these cascades are the namesake for the area. In fact, the area namesake was a cedar staircase built 1890 by one of the first Euro-American

expedintions to explore the Olympics. They used it to cross over a dangerous stretch of rapids. There are a number of hiking trails in this area as well as a campground.

Dosewallips

Finally, on the park's eastern side is Dosewallips, a forested area with a campground that sits next to the Dosewallips River. Several trails are here, including some that lead into the park's interior. At press time, a portion of the road to Dosewallips was washed out (and has been challenging to fix), making car travel impossible 5 miles before the campground and ranger station. Check for road updates before you go.

◀ *Graves Creek in the Quinault*

Get Going:
Activities in the park

If you've read the previous chapters, hopefully they've inspired you to get out and experience the park. There are a number of ways you can do so, and taking a short walk or hike is a good place to start.

Hiking and Backpacking

Whether it's in the forests, on the coast, or in the mountains of Olympic National Park, it's rare when even a brief hike or walk does not yield rewards. Many areas are crowded with people, but other areas see few hikers even in the peak summer season. With 611 miles of trail in the park, there are plenty of places where solitude can be found. Backpacking is also extremely popular, and in 2005

◀ *A view of the Elwha River near the Altair Campground*

nd 31,000 people stayed overnight
e park's backcountry, including
e who enjoy the novelty of camping
ne wild coast. If you want to stay
night, it's necessary to get a permit
 the park's Wilderness Informa-
Center in Port Angeles. You should
p at a preestablished backcountry
in order to limit human impact
n the park. But don't worry, these
 are numerous. Proper storage of
 is strongly recommended as well,
er using bear wires or bear-resistant
sters.

mping

e are sixteen campgrounds within
park, some more primitive than
rs, and four only offer pit toilets

(Deer Park, Graves Creek, North Fork,
and Ozette). Some also only offer full
amenities in the peak season (late spring
through early fall) and may close entirely
during other times of the year. (*NOTE:*
There are no hookups for RVs in any
of the park-operated campgrounds.)
There are no showers in the park campgrounds, but they're sometimes available in areas near the park boundaries.
The current average cost for a campsite
is $12 per night. Kalaloch Campground
is the only campground directly on the
beach, and for that reason it's the most
popular. It's also the only park campground that uses a reservation system in
the summer (www.recreation.gov).

So which campgrounds are best? It
depends on what you're looking for, and
all of them have their charms. In general,

s on the Grand Ridge Trail

Popular and Suggested Hikes in Olympic National Park

Listed below are highlights of some of the more well-traveled trails in the park. An asterisk (*) indicates a wheelchair-accessible trail, and a double asterisk (**) indica a trail that is accessible with assistance. Finally, a triple asterisk (***) indicates that the trail is in the Olympic National Forest, rather than in the national park.

	LENGTH (MILES)	CHALLENGE	FEATURES
Hurricane Ridge			
Big Meadow	0.25 one way	Easy	Spring/summer wildflowers, view of Strait of Juan Fuca, interpretive signs
Hurricane Hill	1.6 one way	Moderate	Spring/summer wildflowers, paved trail, interpret signs, mountain views
Klahhane Ridge	3.8 one way	Moderate	Spring/summer wildflowe mountain views

	LENGTH (MILES)	CHALLENGE	FEATURES
er Park/			
struction Point			
nd Ridge Trail	7.4 one way	Strenuous	Spring/summer wildflowers; views of mountains, lakes, and Strait of Juan de Fuca
rt of the Hills			
rt of the Forest	2.0 one way	Easy	Old-growth forest, big trees, creeks
ha			
lison Falls *	0.1 one way	Easy	Waterfall
nes Ranch Loop	6.0 loop	Moderate	Old-growth forest, historic ranch and cabin, Goblin's Gate site, Elwha River views
mpic Hot Springs	2.5 one way	Easy	Forest, paved trail, hot springs

	LENGTH (MILES)	CHALLENGE	FEATURES
Elwha River/ North Fork Quinault	44.0 one way	Moderate	Old-growth forest, Elwha River views, historic homesteads, crosses park from north to south (average hiking time five days)
Lake Crescent Marymere Falls (partially **)	0.9 one way	Easy	Old-growth forest, creek, trees, waterfall
Spruce Railroad	4.0 one way	Easy	Historic railroad bed, lake views, bicycles allowed
Mount Storm King	2.2 one way	Strenuous	Forests, views of Lake Crescent from above

	LENGTH (MILES)	CHALLENGE	FEATURES
Duc			
Duc Falls	0.8 one way	Easy	Old-growth forest, creeks, waterfall
h Divide/ en Lakes Basin	18.2 loop	Strenuous	Old-growth forest, meadows, lakes, views of Mount Olympus
th Coast			
Shi Beach	3.3 one way	Moderate	Ocean views, sea stacks
nt of the Arches	4.0 one way	Moderate	Ocean views, sea stacks, arches, tide pools
tte			
tte Loop	9.0 loop	Easy	Ocean views, coastal forest, boardwalk, tide pools, petroglyphs

	LENGTH (MILES)	CHALLENGE	FEATURES
Mora/La Push			
Hole-in-the-Wall	1.5 one way	Easy	Ocean views, sea stacks, tide pools, arch
Second Beach	0.8 one way	Easy	Ocean views, sea stacks
Third Beach	1.4 one way	Easy	Ocean views, sea stacks
Hoh			
Hall of Mosses	0.8 round-trip	Easy	Rain forest, big trees, interpretive signs
Spruce Nature (partially **)	1.2 round-trip	Easy	Rain forest, big trees, Hoh River views
Hoh River	17.3 one way	Moderate	Rain forest, approach to Mount Olympus, views of Mount Olympus near end

	LENGTH (MILES)	CHALLENGE	FEATURES
loch			
y Beach	0.2 one way	Easy	Sea stacks, tide pools, ocean views
ch 1	0.1 one way	Easy	Spruce burls, ocean views
ault			
le Glade **	0.5 loop	Easy	Rain forest
ner			
estead **	1.3 loop	Easy	Homestead, rain forest
ault Rain			
st #854 ***	0.6 loop	Easy	Rain forest, interpretive signs
case			
case Rapids	2.0 loop	Easy	Old-growth forest, views of Skokomish River's North Fork, big cedar tree

the Sol Duc, Altair, Kalaloch, and Ozette campgrounds seem to reach capacity most often during the summer—but this might be a function of location rather than quality. The Heart of the Hills campground is the closest to Port Angeles.

Boating

All of the park's major lakes are great for canoeing, kayaking, rowboating, or powerboating. Winds can be strong on Lake Ozette, and this, as well as any other potentially dangerous conditions (such as the weather, large rocks, or strong tides at other locations) should be considered before you embark. Lake Crescent and Lake Quinault are probably the safest for beginners and those seeking casual recreation. Numerous locations rent canoes, kayaks, and other

vessels; however, canoeing or kayak the Elwha and other rivers can be qu dangerous and is only recommende experienced and well-informed boat Popular places outside of the park to explore by water include Freshwater Dungeness National Wildlife Refuge, Discovery Bay. Olympic Raft and Kay (888-452-1443; www.raftandkayak.c rents equipment and also guides trip in a variety of places within and outs of the park. Guided rafting trips are available for both beginners and mo advanced paddlers on the Elwha and Hoh Rivers, as well as the Sol Duc Ri in winter.

Biking

Other than on the roads, there really aren't many places to bicycle in the

Canoeing and kayaking are popular activities on Lake Cre

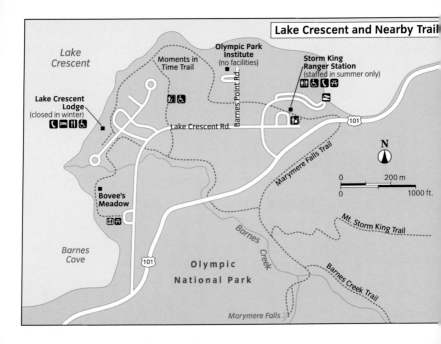

only trail in the park that allows bicy-
is the 4-mile Spruce Railroad Trail, on
Crescent's north side. Some of the
aved roads in the Elwha and Quinault
as may also make for scenic rides, as
as the Obstruction Point Road in the
intains. Be careful to watch for cars.
those who are truly conditioned for
rious ride, the journey up and down
winding 17-mile Hurricane Ridge
d is surprisingly popular. It's rare
ake a summer drive up to the ridge
not see a few impressive individu-
pedaling away. The uphill grade is
roximately 7 percent. Places outside
he park for bicycling include the
npic Discovery Trail that goes from
Angeles to Sequim and also the
int Mueller (near Lake Crescent) and
thills Trails (near Port Angeles).

Fishing

With so many creeks, rivers, lakes, and
a huge ocean, there is no shortage of
places to fish in the park. Regulations are
extensive and are based on location and
population judgments. Check www.nps
.gov/olym/fishing.htm for current information and updates. Washington State
fishing licenses are not required, unless
fishing on the coast. A Washington Catch
record is required if you're fishing for
salmon or steelhead.

Winter Activities

Cross-country skiing is possible on some
trails and roads in areas of the park
where snow falls in the winter. While
there are several locations amenable to
snowshoeing or skiing, the discussion

here will focus on Hurricane Ridge as it is the primary area where these activities occur. Park staff sometimes offer guided interpretive programs from the visitor center on weekends in the winter. A downhill ski slope is operated by a concessionaire, and a snow play area delights those who like the rushing feel of riding down a slope via sled. *NOTE:* The road to Hurricane Ridge closes in winter when weather conditions make travel unsafe. At times heavy traffic volume also demands that people wait below until there is space to accommodate another vehicle in the Hurricane Ridge parking area.

Photographing the Forests

Taking quality photographs in the park's forests can be challenging because of lighting conditions, shadows, and spatial arrangements. For better photographs, try to photograph people from a distance to show their relative height compared to tall trees. Also use an opening in the forest, such as one created by a trail, to center your photographs and create a frame with the trees—this will help compensate for the lighting and spatial indistinctiveness of the park's lush forests.

Just for Families

There are many activities in the park that work well for families, and one of the best is the interpretive programs offered in the summer and early fall. For a schedule of ranger-led programs, pick up a copy of the park newspaper, *The Bugler.* For the young (and the young at heart), there is a Junior Ranger Program with fun activities and information ($1 donation suggested per program for all ages). Those who complete the program receive a badge and certificate.

As for family-friendly trails in the park, the Hoh Rain Forest loop trails, Marymere Falls, and Sol Duc Falls all delight, and the coast has a lot to offer as well. It's hard to find anyone not pleased to watch tide pools and see how many small creatures they can see in the water. With a little bit of explanation about how these animals feed, everyone will be enthralled.

Where Can I See Tide Pools in the Park?

There are many places on the coast where you can see tide pools. Some of the easier places to reach in the park are Hole-in-the-Wall near Rialto Beach, Beach 4 at Kalaloch, and an area directly to the south of Ruby Beach at Kalaloch. Outside the park, Salt Creek County Park also has some tide pools but is located on the Strait of Juan de Fuca. Make sure that you check tide schedules to optimize your arrival during low tide; during high tide the pools might not be visible or safe to reach. Schedules are posted in the park and are available in local phone books. Please don't touch tide pool creatures for their safety and your own, and please respect that many tribes still harvest from the pools as a traditional cultural practice.

Both Lake Crescent and Lake Quinault are great places for families to swim, or to rent a canoe or boat. At Lake Crescent there is a public beach located on the east side, known as East Beach, and a beach on the south known as Bovee's Meadow. There are no lifeguards. There are also places for water entry in the Olympic National Forest at Lake Quina. Of course, Sol Duc Hot Springs is also favorite with families.

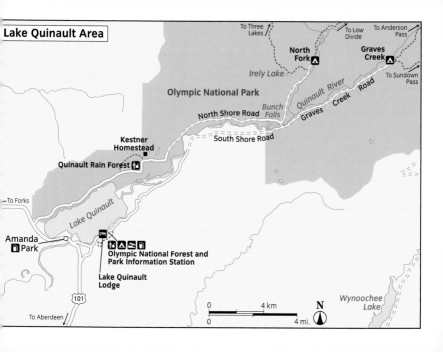

Lake Quinault Area

To Three Lakes

To Low Divide

To Anderson Pass

North Fork

Graves Creek

Irely Lake

To Sundown Pass

Olympic National Park

North Shore Road

Bunch Falls

Quinault River

Graves Creek Road

South Shore Road

Kestner Homestead

Quinault Rain Forest

To Forks

Lake Quinault

Amanda Park

Olympic National Forest and Park Information Station

Lake Quinault Lodge

101

To Aberdeen

0   4 km

0   4 mi.

N

Wynoochee Lake

Hey Ranger! Q&A Just for Kids

Hey, kids! Do you ever have questions about the park that your parents can't answer? Then ask a ranger! They might know the answer. Here are some common questions and answers.

Q. I'm scared of bears. They won't hurt me, will they?

A. Bears don't tend to be interested in us unless we provoke them or threaten them. In fact, they're probably more scared of us than we are of them! To keep safe, travel in the park with other people and store your food properly. If you see a bear, do several things: keep your distance, make some noise to let the bear know your group is around (bears, just like us, might act defensive if surprised), and, most importantly, enjoy!

Q. I've heard about flying squirrels. Where can I see them, and do they really fly?

A. Flying squirrels are nocturnal, meaning that they tend to come out at night, so you probably won't see them. They don't actually fly, but they have a lining of fur between their bodies and legs that allows them to jump and hang glide between trees. They can sometimes "fly" up to 250 feet—about the length of a football field! When they land on a tree, they quickly run to the other side to escape any potential predators, such as spotted owls, that might be on the prowl.

Q. Just how big are the tall trees in the park?
A. The park's older trees can be up to 1,000 years old. When they have this much time to grow they can get quite large. In fact, some of the tallest individual trees in the United States among various tree species live in the park. For instance, the three tallest western hemlocks in the United States are in Olympic National Park! They are each around 172 feet tall and 335 inches in circumference (the distance around the tree's base). The largest grand fir in the park is 246 feet tall and 229 inches in circumference. The largest subalpine fir in the world is also here, and it's 125 feet tall and 252 inches in circumference!

Recharge:
Places to sleep and eat

Within Olympic National Park there are several places you can stay and eat (in addition to the campgrounds, which are covered in the Get Going chapter). The lodging is quite popular and books up early, so reserve ahead of time. There are also many places available outside the park for lodging and food (see the Beyond the Borders chapter).

The Hurricane Ridge Area

While there is no lodging in the Olympic Mountains, there is a snack bar located within the gift shop at the bottom of the Hurricane Ridge visitor center. This small eatery is generally open daily 10:00 a.m. to 6:00 p.m. from late May until early October. American

The Kalaloch Lodge

fast-food-type fare is sold here (approximately $6–$10 per person), as well as the oh-so-popular soft-serve ice cream. There is seating inside the visitor center, but most people prefer to dine outside, enjoying the splendid views on the terrace or eating while listening to a ranger talk.

Lake Crescent

There are two places to stay at Lake Crescent that are officially located within the park: Log Cabin Resort and its campground, and Lake Crescent Lodge. Log Cabin Resort (360-928-3325; www.log cabinresort.net), on the lake's north side, is a beautiful place to relax, swim, and enjoy the view. The atmosphere here is casual and family oriented (expect happy kids running about), and many families return year after year. The resort offers an assortment of rustic motel rooms and cabins that currently range from about $55 to $145 per night depending on the unit. Many of these rooms and cabins accommodate groups of four or more, and pets are allowed for an extra charge of around $12. The resort is open from late May until early September. The campground, adjacent to the lodge's cabins, has accommodations for RVs and tent campers, and fees range from about $16 to $23.

A dining room overlooks the lake and serves breakfast and dinner (breakfast: $8 per adult; dinner: $10 to $30 per adult). There is also a soda fountain/ snack bar (open in the afternoons) and a small grocery store/gift shop. You can rent small boats and canoes from the

The view from Lake Crescent Lodge's pe

resort or pay a fee to launch your own boat. Park ranger programs are usually offered several nights a week at a small amphitheater overlooking the lake.

Lake Crescent Lodge (360-928-3211; www.lakecrescentlodge.com) is on the lake's south side and, like the Log Cabin Resort, offers a great environment for relaxing and enjoying the clear waters of the lake. The lodge's interior is decorated beautifully, and a porch with comfy chairs is a visitor favorite. President Franklin Roosevelt stayed here during his trip to the Olympic Peninsula in 1937, a year before he helped sponsor the legislation that created the national park. A popular trail leads from the lodge through the forest to Marymere Falls. When comparing Log Cabin Resort to Lake Crescent Lodge, most people would generally say this is the quieter place

(they probably mean fewer kids runnin freely), although there are still many families who stay here. There are room inside the lodge, as well as adjacent cottages and motel rooms. Prices rang from about $85 to $200 a night, and p are allowed for an extra charge of arou $12. The lodge is open from early May mid-October.

A dining room serves breakfast, lunch, and dinner (dinner reservations required; breakfast and lunch $10–$20 per adult, dinner $15–$30 per adult). A small coffee bar, open from about noo until 10:00 p.m., is located in the lodge primary room, and an adjacent gift sho is open during the day. The lodge rents small boats for a fee. Park rangers offe programs several nights a week at a sr amphitheater, although chilly winds ca sometimes lead to changes in location

On the west side of Lake Crescent
can stock up on supplies at the
holme Store (360-928-3020), located
r Fairholme Campground. They sell
ceries and rent boats, canoes, and
aks. The store is generally open from
0 a.m. to 7:00 p.m. from late May to
y September.

e Sol Duc Area

Sol Duc Hot Springs Resort (360-
-3583; www.visitsolduc.com) is
ell-known spot among most park
ors: The appeal and relative novelty
ot springs inspires a certain level of
gue. As early as the 1880s, locals
de the journey here to enjoy the hot
er from the springs and benefit from
otential "curative" powers. A luxury
rt opened in 1912 but burned down

only four years later. Later incarnations
of hotel operations followed, and today
the resort rents a variety of lodge rooms
and cabins (ranging from $135–$285
per night; pets are allowed for an extra
charge of around $12). A campground
adjacent to the cabins, primarily for large
RVs, is operated by the lodge; the fee is
about $23 (water and electricity hookups
are available). Another campground,
operated by the national park, is within
walking distance, and a trail leads
from the resort to both campgrounds.
(Campfire programs led by park staff
are offered at the national-park-owned
campground several nights a week.)
The hot springs themselves look little
different than modern swimming pools,
and the water flows through at varying
temperatures in each of the three pools.
Park visitors who aren't staying at the

lodge can pay a fee between $8 and $11 to use the pools.

The resort has a restaurant open in the summer (May–September) that serves breakfast and dinner (prices are approximately $10–$30 per adult). A poolside deli is open from late morning to late afternoon, and a gift shop is located near the front desk. The lodge is open from late March to late October.

The Olympic Coast

Within the coastal region of the park, the Kalaloch Lodge (866-525-2562; www .visitkalaloch.com) is the only official park-sponsored lodging available. The lodge overlooks the ocean and is largely on its own in this geographic area, aside from the national park campground and park buildings. Cabins, motel rooms, and lodge rooms are available year-round

(ranging from $113 to $ 289 a night). A restaurant serves breakfast, lunch, an dinner (breakfast and lunch: $10–$20 per adult; dinner: $20–$30 per adult); small grocery store sells supplies; and a gift shop is located in the main lodge Ranger-led programs often start from right outside the lodge's doors.

Lake Quinault Area

While the Lake Quinault Lodge (360-28 2900; www.visitlakequinault.com) is technically not in Olympic National Pa (it's in Olympic National Forest, on the lake's east side), from a visitor's persp tive it merits discussion here. The lodg sits right on the lake, and just across t street there are trails leading through rain forests of the national forest. Nur ous types of lodge rooms are available year-round (ranging from $70 to $202

Quinault Lodge

night based on season). A restau-
 serves breakfast, lunch, and dinner
 roximately $10–$30 per adult), and
 e is a gift shop. Canoes, kayaks,
and rowboats are available for rent, and
there is a heated pool. National forest
rangers lead regular programs that start
from areas near the lodge.

Beyond the Borders:
Off-site places to sleep, eat, and go

Port Angeles Area

The primary gateway community to Olympic National Park is the city of Port Angeles, where the park's largest visitor center and headquarters are located. For a city that sees so many tourists and travelers each year, Port Angeles (called PA by locals) has a surprisingly pleasant, nonkitschy, and noncommercialized feel to it. Despite how laid-back things seem, the people who live in Port Angeles have a lot of community pride. Colorful murals by local artist Cory Ench adorn buildings, depicting the Olympic Peninsula's beautiful natural landscapes while also paying tribute to the area's cultural history. There are numerous cultural events offered in Port Angeles during the year, with more occurring during the summer

A sand sculpture from the Arts in Action festival in Port Angeles

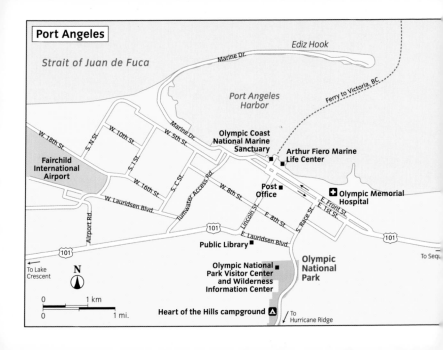

nths. Examples of events include a
ular series of popular concerts on
 pier featuring regional musicians, a
dnesday and Saturday farmer's mar-
, and an annual Arts in Action festival
t includes the only North American
ster Sand Sculpture invitational
petition.

An abundance of restaurants special-
in top-notch ethnic cuisine in addition
eafood and typical American fare.
ile there are restaurants throughout
t Angeles, those that are more well
wn are on or near Front or First
et in the heart of downtown. Some
he best include Thai Peppers, India
n, Bella Italia, Downriggers (seafood),
Dynasty Chinese Restaurant, and
hwhackers (seafood).

Some places you may want to visit
enjoyment include a small but pleas-

ant aquarium, the Arthur Fiero Marine
Life Center; a separate but nearby
Olympic Coast Discovery Center, which
focuses on the Olympic Coast National
Marine Sanctuary; a strip of land, or
"spit," that juts out into the water in Port
Angeles Harbor known as Ediz Hook; and
Salt Creek County Park, where you can
see tide pools and a historic fort after
only a forty-five-minute drive.

Lodging

A wealth of lodging is available in the
Port Angeles area. For other choices in
addition to the hotels provided here, visit
www.portangeles.org.

Red Lion Hotel (221 North Lincoln
Street; 877-333-2733; www.redlion
portangeles.com). Located right next to
the water in downtown Port Angeles, the
Red Lion commands the best location of

any Port Angeles hotel. It is within easy walking distance to the action downtown, and many rooms have views of the Strait of Juan de Fuca. The Crabhouse Restaurant is located in the hotel, and there is a small outdoor swimming pool. Rooms are $110–$180 per night depending on the season.

Best Western Olympic Lodge (140 Del Guzzi Drive; 360-452-2993; www.bestwesternwashington.com). The Best Western is one of Port Angeles's nicer hotels, but unfortunately, it's not within easy walking distance of downtown and doesn't have a view of the water. If these things are less important to you, then the nice rooms, heated pool, and breakfast buffet make it a good place to stay. Standard rooms are about $130 per night; more deluxe rooms are slightly more expensive.

Quality Inn Uptown (101 East Second Street; 360-457-9434; www .choicehotels.com). Located in downtown Port Angeles, the Quality Inn is within short walking distance of restaurants and shops. Only some rooms have water views, and they tend to be more expensive. Rates vary from $80 to $17 based on the room and season.

The Sequim Area

Seventeen miles east of Port Angeles the much talked-about city of Sequim (pronounced as "Squim," not "See-Quim"). Its main claim to fame is the abundant year-round sunshine. Because of a phenomenon known as a "rain shadow" that is cast by the Olympic Mountains, there is only an average of to 17 inches of rain each year in Sequi and relatively few cloudy days. Sequim

also known for its lavender farms, and you'll often see references that you're the lavender capital of the United States. A serious effort began in the 90s to preserve the area's agricultural heritage by growing a signature plant, and lavender was the choice. A herd of wild Olympic elk also live in the Sequim area, and many people see the herd as a source of pride and identity for the community. A few notable natural places to visit in the Sequim area are the Dungeness River Audubon Center that adjoins a pleasant Railroad Bridge Park and a nearby Dungeness National Wildlife Refuge. Near to Sequim is the town of Dungeness, from which Dungeness crabs probably received their name. A classic seafood restaurant in Dungeness known as The Three Crabs has excellent food and a view of the bay.

Sequim's Railroad Bridge Park

There are a considerable number of lodging possibilities in the Sequim area; see www.sequim.com.

Western and Southern Park Areas

The western areas of the Olympic Peninsula have a lot to offer and contain the coastal and rain forest areas of Olympic National Park. The Makah Indian Reser-

vation is a popular destination for those who want to walk out to Cape Flattery (the most northwest place in the contiguous United States) and access one of the national park's most written-about coastal locations, Shi Shi Beach. The Makah also have a museum that focuses on the tribe's culture and their role in the area's history.

The town of Forks is the hub for the western areas of the peninsula and Olympic National Park, and it and surrounding areas offer numerous lodging and camping possibilities, food, and services (see www.forkswa.com). The Quileute Indian Reservation and the town of La Push, near Forks and bordering the national park, offer lodging, camping, and places to buy food and supplies.

For food, you can find tasty seafood at the River's Edge Restaurant, right next to the ocean in La Push. From the restaurant's large windows you can often see bald eagles hunting for fish and harbor seals popping their heads up out of the water. For those visiting the southern side of the park and peninsula, the town of Hoodsport (www.hoodsportwa.com) offers lodging and camping, and so do the Quinault area (www.forkswa.com).

Lodging

Dew Drop Inn (100 Fern Hill Road; 360-374-4055; www.dewdropinnhotel.com) This Forks hotel is family owned and has nice rooms ranging from $55 to $65.

Ocean Park Resort at La Push (330 Ocean Drive; 360-374-5267; www.ocean-park.org). Located on the Quileute Reservation and near to several park beaches, Ocean Park Resort offers an appealing array of rustic but nicely

nished motel rooms, cabins, and
plexes ranging from $30 to $225
epending on type and size of lodging,
d if it has an ocean view).

ospitals, Post Offices,
braries, and Places to
hower

spitals and Walk-in Clinics
mpic Memorial Hospital, 939 Caroline
  Street, Port Angeles; (360) 417-7000
icare, 621 East Front Street, Port
  Angeles; (360) 452-4000
ks Community Hospital, 530
  Bogachiel Way, Forks; (360) 374-6271

st Offices
East First Street, Port Angeles
South Sunnyside Avenue, Sequim
South Shore Road, Quinault

76 North Lake Cushman Road,
  Hoodsport
61 South Spartan Avenue, Forks
500 Ocean Drive, La Push

Libraries
2210 South Peabody Street, Port
  Angeles
171 Forks Avenue South, Forks
630 North Sequim Avenue, Sequim

Places to Shower
Bogachiel State Park
Salt Creek County Park
Dungeness Recreation Area
William Shore Memorial Pool, Fifth and
  Lincoln, Port Angeles
YMCA, 302 South Francis Street, Port
  Angeles

Resources

Northwest Interpretive Association (164 South Jackson Street, Seattle, WA 98104; 877-874-6775 [customer service]; www.nwpubliclands.org). A nonprofit organization that operates the bookstores within Olympic National Park.

Friends of Olympic National Park (P.O. Box 2438, Port Angeles, WA 98362; www.friendsonp.org). This organization's mission is to preserve the park's resources and promote understanding of the park's importance.

Olympic Park Institute (111 Barnes Point Road, Port Angeles, WA 98363; 360-928-3720; www.yni.org/opi). Located at Lake Crescent, the institute offers outdoor-education programs.

Peninsula Daily News (305 West First St., P.O. Box 1330, Port Angeles, WA 98362; 360-452-2345; www.peninsula dailynews.com). The primary newspap for the Port Angeles area.

Olympic National Forest (1835 Black Lake Boulevard Southwest, Olym pia, WA 98512; 360-956-2402; www.fs .fed.us/r6/olympic). Olympic National Forest borders Olympic National Park and offers numerous trails and campin opportunities.

The Mountaineers (300 Third Avenue West, Seattle, WA 98119; 206-284-8484; www.mountaineers.org). A club that organizes outdoor activities i and around Washington.

Olympic Coast National Marine Sanctuary (115 Railroad Avenue East, Suite 301, Port Angeles, WA 98362; 36 457-6622; www.olympiccoast.noaa.gc The marine sanctuary protects the oce and marine life off the Olympic Coast.

Photos by Levi T. Novey except pp. 3, 34: Marco Carbone; p. 7: U.S. Fish and Wildlife Service/photo by David Men▮ p. 24: photo courtesy Olympic National Park; p. 25: U.S. Fish and Wildlife Service/photo by John and Karen Hollingsworth; pp. 29, 54: Peter Gleason; pp. 30, 39, 44: Paula Sprenger; p. 33: U.S. Fish and Wildlife Service/photo by Karen Laubenstein; pp. 35, 75: Elizabeth Hunt; p. 48: Chad Goodchild; p. 63: Royce Rogers

Text design by Mary Ballachino
Maps created by XNR Productions, Inc. © Morris Book Publishing, LLC

Library of Congress Cataloging-in-Publication Data is available.
ISBN 978-0-7627-4807-5

Printed in China
10 9 8 7 6 5 4 3 2 1